PACKAGE LIKE A PRO

Reporting for international news media:
how to get your stories published
on major TV news networks.

By Adesewa Josh

AUTHOR'S NOTE

Hi, I'm Adesewa Josh, and I'm going to be leading this course on how to *Package Like a Pro*.

The course is about teaching journalists how to write and produce news packages for international broadcast news media, a skill in high demand across the globe. I know from experience that it's really difficult for journalists to find the opportunities to be trained in this skill. But this is why I have produced this course, to provide you with the tips and tricks to help you get started or to perfect what you already know. I'll teach you some of the skills that transformed my career from a local journalist in Africa to becoming the creator and anchor of one of the top three current affairs programs on a fast-rising global news network.

Before we begin, let me share some more about myself and my experience as a news correspondent and producer.

I started my journalism career in 2012, in my home country Nigeria, rising to the position of a morning show host and a news anchor on one of Africa's best-known TV networks, *Channels Television*. I'd been a TV presenter for half a decade prior to that. I have a Master's degree in politics and global affairs from the Columbia School of Journalism in New York. I presented and co-produced the Emmy-nominated United Nations TV program *21st Century* between 2015 and 2017. I've since received both regional and international recognition for my work.

I'm currently based in Istanbul as the creator, senior producer, and presenter of *Africa Matters* on *TRT World*, Turkey's first English-language international news channel. After nearly two decades of being a broadcast journalist across three continents, I've noticed it can be difficult for international news networks to find skilled freelance reporters in regions where their coverage is limited... especially reporters who can deliver quality news packages. A good example is Africa.

Regional reporters – as I like to describe them – are vital to international newsrooms because they have the advantage of getting to the story first, even before a big network correspondent has a chance to arrive. They also have a unique opportunity, not only to own their story as local experts and pitch underreported stories, but to lead the narrative by being able to respond quickly. Often, freelance reporters are the ONLY source of news-gathering where access is limited.

In this course, you'll learn how to put a news story together and become the go-to source for television packages on the stories happening around you. *Package Like A Pro* will help you turn your newsgathering hobby into a money-making gig.

ACKNOWLEDGEMENTS

To Sarah Balter and Tehmina Qureshi who made this project possible.

INTRODUCTION

Broadcast news is made up of either packaged content or live reports. A packaged news story is one that is researched, filmed, edited and broadcasted after the event has happened. The word 'package' refers to a complete product, and there's a well-defined process to be followed, all of which is covered in this course.

I created this course because I want to encourage more people from all over the world, especially from remote and hard-to-reach regions, to produce news stories. I want to help them understand how to use journalism skills and ethics to give their stories that edge that appeal to international broadcasters and their audiences. If you are a fresh journalism graduate and want to quickly master the art of news packages, then this course is perfect for you. However, this course is equally useful for content creators, writers and video journalists hoping to hone their broadcast skills and rise within their newsrooms.

You'll learn what makes a good news story, how to hook international news media into airing your story, how to write and voice a script, and how to film a signature Piece-To-Camera. Let's begin!

MODULE 1: THE SCIENCE OF STORYTELLING

We'll begin with what a story is and what makes it newsworthy. A news story educates, informs, investigates, and sometimes, entertains. It usually doesn't have a happy ending, but sometimes, it does. Above all, a news story must be based on facts, or it will be misleading and most likely will not make the cut of stories bring aired.

Generally, a news story is what happens when characters interact within some kind of conflict. The stories as told by reporters are usually based on their experiences and difficulties, with the finer points of the plot unveiling the knots of the conflict vis a vis the characters' roles and goals. What a reporter does is observe, collect details, and write them down with the aim of replaying it for a larger audience. All of these processes require certain techniques for making your observations, detailing and recounting of them more credible and interesting.

Types of stories
There are several kinds of news stories, including breaking news (also called straight news), human interest stories (also known as features), and other formats for business and sports. All of these stories have a different style, but they're all based on factual evidence and must be stitched together to rise to the same level of interest. When looking for a good story, look for events and people with a wide impact. International broadcasters are not looking for local or national news. The story has to have something to spark international interest. They can be earthquakes, wars, human rights issues, politics, diplomacy, culture, art, food, celebrities,

leaders and governments, and much more.

The world of news is massive, so you'll want to find your own focus or niche, called "beat" in journalistic lingo. If a lot that's internationally interesting happens in your area, it would make sense to specialize in that. For example, a reporter from Gaza, Palestine, may be stuck where they are, but they would have an endless supply of stories of international interest. They can use this situation to provide their people with public service as owners of their own narrative. The same goes for reporters in Africa, Europe, and Asia. There is little doubt that a skilled regional reporter can do a much better job producing a story from their own country than most foreign journalists.

Why do we tell stories?
We tell stories to inform and to reveal what's happening in the public interest. We warn of danger, connect cultures, humanize a problem, and the people involved in them. We help audiences understand more about what's going on in the world around them. A good international reporter tells a story in several contexts, but puts the regional (or local) context first and then helps an international audience see why they should care. Stories can also convince viewers that something matters. But it actually has to matter.

An international flight gone missing, or crashed, is something of global interest. The coronavirus pandemic, terror attacks, a coup, an occupation, violent mass street protests, a sudden and significant dip or flight in cryptocurrency or gold prices, are all subjects with the potential to resonate with a global audience. Moreover, stories of human achievements, about people surviving against all odds and triumphing in the face of adversity, are also themes that have become popular across many newsrooms. Often, even if a story is local but is way out of the ordinary, it also evokes global interest.
So always ask yourself, why am I telling this story? Will people on the other side of the world be interested in hearing about it? Does

it provide some answers to a global problem or shed more light on it? What am I getting at? Because a successful story must ask and answer questions while keeping the audience asking for more.

What makes a story a journalistic piece?
Every Tom, Dick and Harry can tell stories, and social media proves this. We're in the age of a storytelling explosion, where anyone can post or tweet about an idea that goes viral.
But a journalistic piece has gone through a process of verification, analysis, balance, and objectivity. It's produced and reported with responsibility for the truth and accountability to the characters.
Journalism is the responsible sharing of information and every journalist should be accountable for, and committed to, telling the truth…no matter what.
But to do your characters justice, you have to be able to empathize with them enough to gain understanding alongside the details.

Empathy is the ability to sense and imagine what others are thinking or feeling. Use empathy while you're recording and relating the experiences of your characters. Great reporting actually moves an audience to empathize with the characters too. This is especially helpful with a call to action or caution. There's some really interesting science behind why stories can be a good way to foster empathy. Researcher Paul Zak found that stories change our behavior by changing our brain chemistry.

In one study, Zak and his team showed a group of volunteers a story about a father and his young son. The son had cancer. The father struggled with the terminal nature of his son's disease. Researchers drew blood from the viewers before and after, and found that watching it caused them to produce two chemicals: cortisol, which focuses our attention on what's important, and oxytocin, which is connected to caring, connection, and empathy.

After they were done with the study, the participants were paid and then given a chance to donate the money to charity. Those with both cortisol and oxytocin in their systems were more likely to donate. The higher the chemical levels, the more money they gave away.

Sensationalism

Sensationalism provokes public interest at the expense of accuracy and ethics. I suggest you avoid it like 'the plague' if you want your stories to be taken seriously.

Not every story you tell will have a magical impact on the public. But desperation for ratings looks obvious to the public and shows you're likely willing to doctor the truth in a way that's self-serving and dangerous. Earning the public's trust is difficult but losing it is easy. A good journalist puts people first and is obsessed with facts balance, fairness, and objectivity.

EXERCISE

1) Ask yourself, why do you want to tell stories?

2) What is the role of empathy in storytelling?
A) To feel good
B) To feel bad
C) To help people understand what others are going through so they can take action

MODULE 2: RESEARCH

Your journey into news packaging begins with research. Experienced reporters build a network of reliable sources for their stories over time, but if you're just starting out, research is the best way to get a lead.

Research is key in the news business. Researching an idea is the process of systematically investigating the details of a story. Reporters have to find out the facts from valid sources, and then evaluate and cross-check their validity. They must be proactive: make calls, visit offices, interview people, read books on the subject, dig online, take meticulous notes, and question authorities to find information wherever it is. Reporters also have to be ready to set aside their own beliefs and comfort zones to get to the facts.

For example, a community or religious leader you're very close to might be embroiled in a corruption scandal. You still need to challenge them. If you are friends with the son of a politician you're investigating, you must still do your job as a journalist.
As an observer and reporter, your personal views do not matter, and they can actually get in the way of your story, if you're not conscious of them.

While research and planning before you go into the field is most important, it doesn't end. Being aware of all of the details is key before, during, and after you've filed your package, because situations can, and often do change. Stories change. Researching will help you stay on top of all the possible angles and adjust when things don't go according to plan.

Even if you've got an interesting story and you've done the research and planning right, don't be surprised if editors and executive producers request more information, make suggestions, or point out holes in your planning. Don't take it personally. You can learn a lot from their experience.

Sources
You want news networks to trust you, to trust your ability to use excellent sources. You don't want them to remember you for using loose or lazy details in your reporting, otherwise they'll never work with you again. Except in rare cases, you are not the primary source of the facts in your story. An exception can be if you're in the field and witnessing something as it happens, on camera. Otherwise, facts come from primary sources which have direct experience of an event, are public, and can agree to an interview.

There are three broad categories of sources: primary, professional, and official.

Primary sources are reliable characters who can provide details and opinions based on their personal experiences in connection with the story you're telling.
For example, refugees or IDPs (internally-displaced persons) in a camp are qualified to talk about life there and can be considered primary sources. They can be nameless VOXPOP (also known as "voice of the people"), reactions at a protest, or statements from characters at the center of your story.

What can be described as a sub-category of primary sources, are the **official primary sources.** These are members of the local or national governments. Police chiefs, lawmakers, and ministers are a few examples. They can also be online studies by ministries, census data and other demographic information on government websites. These provide death, injury, survivor, and other demographic details to support your story. Moreover, at all costs avoid using blogs, fake news, most social media, and op-eds as primary sources.

Professional sources are usually experts in their field. Choose reliable professionals or organizations known as authorities of the information they work with. NGOs, universities, companies, doctors, artists, and athletes are all relevant examples. Reporters often use the UN, NGOs, and human rights groups for figures related to events or living phenomena such as people displaced by war or the number of malnourished people in the world.

Meanwhile, **secondary sources** cite, comment, or build on primary sources. Examples are textbooks that review research, news articles, critiques, and commentaries.

There's another kind of source, the **confidential sources**, and are most relevant for investigative journalists. Confidential sources require extreme care and discretion, because they could be at risk of physical, emotional, and economic harm if their identities are revealed. It can be difficult to get them to agree to an interview but if and when they do decide to go on record, it's often a game-changer for the story you're telling. However, you would need to protect their identity by keeping their name and appearance confidential.

Fact-checking
If research is what you do before setting out to report and write a story, fact-checking is what you do when you're done writing and before you voice your script.

Look for anything that might not make sense. Holes in your logic. Anything that could be based on fake news. Check that the overall impression and direction of your story is sound and that your meaning is clear. Double and triple check anything big, breaking or controversial that could get you banned should it turn out to be wrong.

Don't rely on news articles for figures. Dig deeper to find the report that published the numbers and always cite your source. If a source says something that sounds suspect, look for other sources of the same information. Cross-check where possible. If you know your area, the people, the region…you'll know when something isn't making sense. A good newsroom will fact-check your facts, so make sure they stand up to careful scrutiny.

EXERCISE

1. What is the first step in the process of writing news packages

A) Watching TV
B) Speaking to your neighbor
C) Find a good story

MODULE 3: PITCHING

What is a news pitch? It's a short description of the story you want to tell. It must, at first glance, convince a news editor or producer that it's timely and a good fit for their platform. Pitching your story is like marketing a product. It needs to poke, arouse, and provoke interest. Try to make it impossible for an editor or producer to say no. The following tips will get your pitches noticed faster, even if they're in a pool of a 100 other pitches.

Know the news organization
The reason most freelancers don't hear back from international newsrooms is that the stories they pitch don't fit their platform. Remember, I said earlier that pitching is like marketing? You must know your audience, and that means knowing the platform's audience. For example, a conservative media platform is unlikely to respond to a pitch about gay doctors who just discovered a potential breakthrough in cancer treatment.

It's true that some stories are bigger than platform biases. But I've chosen this example to show you how ignoring a network's branding and values can work against you. An exclusive on a successful cancer treatment would likely be accepted by any platform, regardless of values. If the story is so important, a conservative channel would de-emphasize the sexual preference of the doctor.

On the other hand, a liberal news outlet would most likely buy into the story without question, because gay contributions to society could be incredibly important to their audience. The best way to know a network's values and what they report on is to consume their content. Know what they feed their audience.
Over the years the question I've heard many executive producers

ask is: "Why should we care?"

Don't take it personally. Knowing why is knowing whether you have a good story or not. There are a gazillion stories coming through the wires every day, which can make deciding on where to focus difficult. That's why no matter how international a newsroom gets there's always the tendency to curate news for one audience first and then for the rest. So, ask yourself, "What is the primary audience of the platform I'm pitching to?" and that will help guide your focus and pitch.

Your idea must be authentic, current, and concise
Now that you know where to pitch your story, it's time to think about your idea so you can articulate it well on paper. As I mentioned before, every pitch should be a summary of your story. It is also known as a synopsis.

A good summary communicates your story's essence in one or two sentences. This can be very challenging, because it can be hard to prioritize the most important details. So, focus on the five Ws. Write a sentence, or two, a paragraph of maximum four sentences, which answers the who, what, when, where, why... and sometimes also the how, of your story.

You also want to make sure that a similar story has not already aired on the same news platform. I see this happen a lot with feature pieces. Before you hit send do a quick search of your idea online. Sometimes you may see something similar to your pitch on the air or online and you might need to re-evaluate your story to see if you have an angle that adds additional value. If you don't, try to find one.

For example, if the channel you want to pitch to has already aired a story about young people crowdfunding online to build public toilets in a village in Southern Madagascar, while your story is about how tech increases the chances of fundraising in remote places, you might want to add a new angle to your pitch about how the money is being spent, or how local businesses also benefit as a result. In short, give us something new. After all, we're in the news business!

Have a reporting plan
Producers want to know you've done your homework to be able to tell a credible story. Tell us about the elements we're going to see on the screen. Describe the visual elements, or shots, you plan to use with your story. Remember, it's television, and we're in the business of good pictures, so make sure the visuals are strong, which means they're capable of instantly grabbing our attention.

As you plan, think of the shots that will draw an audience in from the get-go. Give brief details about the environment you plan to shoot for each of your characters. Include locations and keep backups in mind just in case. Also describe interview possibilities, as in who the main characters are likely to be. This will also help you imagine what responses you'll likely be getting during the interview. You won't be too far with your guesses, but if you're completely off course, meaning your story changes or your character says the unexpected, then I'd say go with the flow and report the story just like that. Producing is also about being able to adapt to these changes.

Give an ETA
Timing is everything in the news business. Aside from getting the facts right, getting the story as first, fast, and exclusive as possible is crucial to every 21st-century newsroom. Executive Producers like reporters who can pitch good stories, but that is of no use if they can't meet deadlines. But please don't over-promise! Nothing is worse than a story that's already planned for broadcast coming in late! Not only is it unprofessional, but it could also get you blacklisted. Only promise what you can deliver. Again, if the timing of your pitch is great, and you've summarized your story well, you're likely to get a response. When that happens, the ball is now in your court to deliver a well-researched, well-written, and well-edited story on time. Don't sweat it, the next chapters will

teach you how.

Budgeting

Most international news networks have a fixed prize for news packages. It's important to find out how much, or at least have an idea of the network's rates before you pitch your story so you don't under bill. If you can't figure out the network's going rate for the services you're about to offer, then just ask the producer who is commissioning the package.

In the event that your budget for a story is higher than a network's going rate, then send them a cost breakdown to show them why you're demanding more money. It would be approved, if they want the story badly enough.

EXERCISE

1. Why do you need to research about the news organization before pitching your story?

A) To introduce yourself as a fan
B) To tailor your pitch to the platform's audience
C) To get noticed

2. Write a sample pitch.

TV Sample Pitches

Pitch 1

A DOCTOR IN SOUTH AFRICA HELPS THOUSANDS DISPLACED BY FLOODS

Your name: John Doe
Delivery Date & Time: XX-XX-XX
Format: PKG
Suggested Air Date & Time: XXXXXX
Location(s): Tongaat, Kwa-zulu natal

SYNOPSIS:
Dr. Imtiaz Sooliman, founder of the South African NGO Gift of the Givers, is helping thousands of people weather a deadly storm that's believed to be driven by climate change. More than 40,000 KwaZulu-Natal residents are homeless after more than 300mm of rain fell in a single day. The death toll, now officially 448, is expected to rise as more than 200 people are still missing.
Dr Sooliman is helping thousands of families pick up the pieces in what has been described as the worst floods to have hit the province.

ELEMENTS:
Interview with Dr. Sooliman on the work he's doing on the ground

in the aftermath of the floods. We will see the damage and destruction in various parts of the province in driving shots and in going into areas where homes have been completely destroyed. We will speak to a family that has been left with no home and with children unable to go to school.

Length of shoot: One day
Budget: X$

PITCH 2

WAR IN UKRAINE DISRUPTS UGANDA'S OIL PALM MARKET

Your name: John Doe
Delivery Date & Time: XX-XX-XX
Format: PKG
Suggested Air Date & Time: XXXXXX
Location(s): Kampala & Kalangala

SYNOPSIS:
The prices of commodities have gone up in Uganda over the last four months. Fuel prices are now more than $1.6 dollars for a liter of petrol and being a complementary product, the price of everything else has also risen. This is because the edible oils market, from which cooking oil and soap are made, have been heavily disrupted. Russia and Ukraine are at war and the two European nations control 80 percent of the global sunflower oil trade market.
This is because Uganda doesn't produce enough crude palm oil. However, Ugandan palm oil growers, particularly on the Kalangala islands of Lake Victoria, are looking to make most of the current market shift.

ELEMENTS:
We will film a roadside quick food maker who uses cooking oil to explain how he/she has been affected by the high cooking prices. We will then proceed to film at an oil palm farm and speak to a farmer who is looking to supply more fruits and make more of the

opportunity. We will also speak to an industry professional about the trends of the economy / edible oils market.

Length of shoot: Two days
Budget: X$

MODULE 4: ETHICS AND OBJECTIVITY

I've decided to call this chapter "staying objective" because that's exactly what it takes to be objective. Stay objective. Let's define that word.

Objectivity is not letting your own personal judgments, emotions, and biases influence your reporting. A reporter's personal interest gives them motivation, but reporting in public interest comes with responsibilities. That means including all the perspectives, not just those that are popular or accepted. Reactions must come from the accusers and the accused, the for, the against, from all who lose, and all who benefit.

Being inclusive of every perspective shows you did the work, and care about balance, which is an important indicator of objectivity. Objectivity is not about burying the truth in perspectives, but rather about seeking the truth above all. But there's a paradox regarding objectivity. What you learn in journalism school sometimes does little to prepare you to work objectively in the 'real world'. What they don't teach you is that all newsrooms have their own internal biases, ethical standards, and values. You'll have to decide what your values are and how they align with who you want to work for.

With practice, you will develop ethical editorial judgment. You'll learn where to draw the lines, what to keep in, leave out, and earn the trust of newsrooms and audiences. Here are some key takeaways.

There are several key ethical standards across global news organizations. In essence, they call on journalists to seek the truth, act in the public interest and minimize harm. No matter what language you speak, what race you belong, or what country you reside in, you're held to the following ethical standards as a journalist:

Honesty: You have an obligation to seek out the truth and report it as accurately as possible. This requires diligence which means making every effort humanly possible to seek out all the facts relevant to a story and going the extra mile to corroborate any information with multiple sources.

Independence: You're to avoid taking political sides and should not act on behalf of special interest groups. Any political affiliations or financial investments that might constitute a conflict of interest with the subject of your story should be declared to editors and readers.

Fairness: In addition to being independent, you're to show impartiality and balance in your reporting. Most news stories have more than one side, and you should capture this, even when you disagree. That being said, however, you should avoid placing two different perspectives on equal footing where one is unsupported by evidence.

Minimizing Harm: This is an editorial-level decision as many news organizations believe not every fact that can be published should be published. If harm could come to private individuals — particularly children — as a result of disclosure exceeds the public good that would come of it. Public figures, especially politicians, are an exception to this rule.

Avoiding libel: This is a legal as well as a moral imperative for journalists. You cannot print false or twisted statements about your characters that could damage their reputation. A simple way to avoid libel and protect your work is to double-check your facts.

Proper attribution: You should never plagiarize, which means to take someone's work or idea and pass it off as your own. It's okay to use information or ideas from another media outlet or journalist as long as you attribute it to them.

EXERCISE

1. What is objectivity to you? Do you think it's an unnecessary burden journalists have to bear? Or is it important when telling stories that could shape a community, country, or even the world?

2. What is the best way to stay objective as a reporter

A) Pretend they don't care

B) Avoid bad people

C) To explore all the angles of a story and always keep the people in view.

MODULE 5: INTERVIEWING AND REPORTING

By now you should be able to zero in on a good news story. The next step is to go find your characters and prepare for your interviews.

Knowing who you will interview will help guide your research and your storytelling. At the same time, you can think in terms of story angles. A good story has at least two angles. Usually, in news, the event itself is one angle and the characters another. For example, a chemical company is being sued for negligence. The events that led to the negligence represent one angle. The CEO defending the company is your other angle. A victim of negligence, or even two, can each talk about how they were affected, adding a third angle to the story. Perhaps a lawyer or a government official can talk about the legal implications for the company. Another angle. You need to find these people and get them to talk to you. Use their angles to round out your story and add value. But avoid repetition and frivolous angles just to fill space.

Start by digging through newspaper reports connected to your story. There are bound to be one or two print reporters that have done the same. Local newspapers, especially digitized ones, are a treasure trove of information that can help you identify people to interview. Newspaper archives will also provide background as secondary sources. You can even reach out to the journalist, who wrote the article, with questions. It's a great way to get extra details and to build a network of colleagues whose work you admire and follow. Also search for characters online. Social media and email accounts are also great ways to initiate contact.

Visit the area where your story lives and talk to people to learn more. For a package, you'll eventually work your way towards one or two characters who are central to the story – whose account or perspective drives the narrative of your story. Make sure such characters are directly connected to your story and represent an angle that adds value. Foreign correspondents usually rely on fixers to find such characters for their stories. But just like it takes a trusted reporter to tell a story, it takes a trusted fixer to find good characters. As you develop a sense of editorial judgment, put it good use by double-checking a character's background and suitability.

Take the time to 'pre-interview' your characters. Even if they've agreed to an interview for a live recording, talk to them ahead of time to get a sense of what they'll say and where they're coming from. This will help you come up with interview questions when it's time, while also enabling them to get a sense of you and perhaps trust you, something which is very helpful if the survivors are traumatized.

However, many stories don't have the gift of time, such as protests and natural disasters, but don't worry. You will adapt. Breaking news, for example, almost always tells itself if you're diligent and use good judgment. There's less digging, and the evidence, events, shots and characters are all there. Now let's identify and discuss the elements of a news package.

SOTs (sound on tape)
There are several ways to know if the character you have for your story is good enough. They stand out, express themselves or their experiences reflect an entire group of people in your story. But you need to get those answers on camera. You need SOTs.
SOTs, also known as soundbites, are a very powerful component of any news package.

A great set of SOTs can make writing your story effortless because all you will be doing is filling in the blanks. The shorter the SOTs, the better. They should be no more than 15 to 20 seconds long, and ideally not more than three in a two-minute news package. Incorporating SOTs into a story is a skill that comes with practice, and by knowing your story inside out. But generally, SOTs carry forward the emotional and descriptive impact of the story. An editor will slash adjectives from every part of your script except a SOT.

Characters such as survivors, witnesses or participants of a protest understandably tend to express their experiences emotionally, thus, lending credibility to the importance of reporting on it. Official SOTs, however, are usually not emotional. They also add credibility to your story, but with official information, numbers, and statements.

To get strong SOTs, you've got to prepare good interview questions. Here are a few tips to help you prepare for your interview.

a) Avoid questions with definitive answers. Such as questions that can be answered in a yes, no, or other one-word replies. Instead of asking a refugee or an IDP "are you feeling okay?", or "how are you feeling?" go with "tell me what it's been like to try to make it through the winter in an IDP camp." You want an answer that describes an experience and that you can actually use.

b) Avoid generic or leading questions. Instead of "did you see the police doing anything there?" ask "what did you see the police doing there?"

c) During interviews, make sure you are equipped with a writing pad, camera, and microphone. Notice inconsistencies in timelines, testimonies, and witnesses. Take good notes! When in doubt, ask for clarifications. You are responsible for getting it right. Your writing pad is your best friend.

d) And finally, trust your gut! If you feel something is off, most likely it is.

EXERCISE

1. **Prepare interview questions for the characters in your story pitch.**

2. **What do you do when you notice a character might be giving false testimony?**
A) Call them a liar
B) Call off the interview and hand them over to the police
C) Notice inconsistencies in timelines, testimonies and witnesses, and go back and double-check through secondary sources.

MODULE 6: FILMING

As a rule, you should plan the shoot with your cameraman before you head out to the field. Discuss the shots you want. The characters, conflicts and the interview formats you'd like to explore. This kind of planning gets you both on the same page. As you get used to writing your own scripts, you'll be able to anticipate what you'll want to see in your package and what you'll want to write.

Communication is key.

Once you're certain the cameraman knows what you want, give them the space to use their expertise and get the job done. In time, you'll develop a working relationship and be able to communicate on the go in the field. Always double-check your sound in every environment. Take extra care when filming in a very active area like a protest, environmental disaster or war. Whenever in doubt, ask your cameraman to fix the sound levels, because one of the worst things that can happen to a reporter is to get home with great shots only to discover you've been filming with bad or even no sound.

If you're recording reactions from people in the streets, also known as **voxpops** (or voice of the people), use a handheld mic popularly known as the dynamic microphone, covered with a wind protector. It's always a good idea to use a wind protector on your handheld mic outdoors. It reduces the risk of the "pop" sound getting into your audio and also helps ensure your voice is not 'gone with the wind'. A lapel mic, the one that's clipped to the reporter's shirt is not the best choice in a noisy, active environment, and might make it harder to conduct interviews. It's just easier to point a mic at a protester and roll tape than to ask and wait to get them mic'd up with a clip-on.

Now let's talk about the shots.

You and your cameraman have discussed locations. An experienced cameraman will have a good idea of what shots you will need. But you should also be aware of them too.

Don't forget, the interview is part of your collection of shots. Rely on your cameraman to frame, light and mic the subject. Needless to say, please work with an experienced cameraman!

The most common shot is **b-roll**, or the various shots that show a location. B-roll can come as close-up, mid, wide, panning, and aerial shots. Zoomed shots are not generally used in a news package unless the story is huge and there are no other shots. At times shots taken by the public using camera phones are also used, if the story is big enough.

One of the important features of b-roll is 'nat-sound', or natural sound. The natural sound of a location adds dimension and draws the viewer into the story. Car engines and honking in traffic. Birdsong at a park. People shouting at a protest. It's essential to include this at the beginning, end, and strategically throughout your package. Without sound, it will fall flat, just images with a voiceover.

Another common shot is a **cutaway**. These include the character in the story. The main character of your package is positioned in their home environment or any environment reflective of the issue being talked about. Shoot the character doing whatever's in the plan to best tell the story. Moving around? Shoot them driving, walking, at work, it depends on the story. B-roll and cutaways can be used in every part of a package, including as setups before a SOT, cover for a longer SOT, opening shots, and final shots.

GVs, or general vision, is also a type of b-roll that can help fill out your story. It can keep you from running out of shots. Shoot at least three minutes of general vision shots in relation to your story. For example, a political story would benefit from billboards of politicians, murals, and even campaign posters.

Lastly, let us not forget the **beauty shot**. These are shots of high-profile buildings or iconic locations. The White House at sunset. Stadium aerials during a big game. A wide shot of a rainbow over a majestic waterfall. Don't miss out on the opportunities to use these to add eye-pleasing value to your story.

And I must repeat... natural sound is your best friend! You'll see why during the editing process.

EXERCISE

1) Why is it important to double-check sound when filming?
A) Because you like listening to yourself
B) To confirm sound quality while still on the field
C) Because it's cool

MODULE 7: PTC

A PTC is also known as a piece-to-camera and is part of the package that features you, the producer, in the flesh. While every part of your script should highlight something interesting, add value to your story, and transition well from one part to the next, the PTC is where you get to connect with your audience in an even bigger way. They'll see your personality. They'll get to put a face with the sound of your voice and see who you are. It also proves you were there, in the field, right where the story is going down.

A standard news package of between one-and-a-half, to two-and-a-half minutes, should have only one PTC.
There's hardly any rulebook out there for PTCs, but here are some guidelines to help you make a good one.

Write a good script and make it short and simple.
Before you can write a good PTC, you must have an idea of where your story is leading and where it's likely to end. And sometimes when you're unsure, a good old trick is to write about statistics or published reports that support your story. Another way to go is to tease the story of the character that's coming next in your package. For starters, keep your PTC between three to four lines, or no more than 20 seconds long. Some networks will ask you to submit your PTC for sub before you film it, so make sure you know what the PTC policy of the network you're working with is.

Memorize
This is where the 'keep it short, simple, and straight to the point' principle comes in handy. It saves you the headache of too many takes just because you're struggling to remember what you wrote. And believe me, field reporting leaves you little room for errors or double-takes. If your cameraman is the impatient type, then you

may find yourself in a very uncomfortable situation. Here are a couple of hacks to help you remember your lines:

    a) Read it out loud to yourself 10 times. Then start saying the lines aloud without looking at the script. You may glance at the script when you forget, but pick up from where you fell off.

    b) Voice record your PTC on your phone, and then put it on auto-replay till you're ready to film it. This also allows your subconscious to absorb the lines.

Filming your PTC
PTCs are generally shot outdoors, but the environment where you choose to film your PTC must fit with your story. This means if your story is about toilets, then it makes sense to film your PTC in a restroom. Think creatively about how to add value to your story with the location you choose. Make a strategic choice. The best visuals are the most relevant to your story. A bad location will only be distracting.

If you're covering a protest and choose to film inside the crowd, be smart enough to rehearse your steps with your cameraman, and also do a proper security inventory before taking your PTC. Otherwise, a safe distance from the crowd will also drive home the point of your story.

Fewer hand gestures are better
Please use hand gestures sparingly. It's natural to use 'the hand' while talking, but some people use them in every sentence they speak. Please avoid that. There's something weird about waving your hands all over your face on camera. It's distracting. My favorite journalist in the TV news industry — Christiane Amanpour — rarely uses her hands while reporting. But you can tell it's something she's mastered over the years because she tends to keep them tucked around her midsection in a way that's controlled, yet looks authentic. You can find her work online and see what I mean.

The best way to keep from waving your hands around dramatically during your PTC is to be aware that it's your mouth that needs to move and produce sound. Not your hands. Also, try to keep your hands around your midsection and out of your face. This is probably why some people prefer to use a handheld mic. But then they have to deal with the other hand that's not holding on to the mic.

You can conservatively and strategically gesture towards important buildings, areas, people, events, and more. You can stand still or sit, or 'walk and talk' when you have more experience. Where safe and appropriate, it's always better to show than to tell. Stand in front of, next to, or walk through, or alongside, your subject. Face the camera as squarely as possible while making gestures. Gestures look great when they highlight, point, or reveal something, and are natural. Don't worry, you'll find your rhythm once you remind yourself that only your mouth needs to do the talking.

Other PTC technicalities
Depending on the environment, a lapel mic is the best way to record your voice for a PTC. It takes away the awkwardness of getting the right posture, a burden that comes with handheld mics. I've seen a lot of good reporters in awful mic-holding postures. If you must use a handheld mic, ensure the following:

  a) Avoid bringing the mic too close to your chin. Avoid holding it like a singer/ rapper, it looks ridiculous on a reporter. Hold it close to your chest but at a considerable distance from your chin. Your cameraman will adjust your sound volume to fit.
  b) Wear plain colors when filming your PTC. Avoid outfits that make you look like a clown. Take a cue from TV anchors, there's a reason why they don't wear plaid on the air. It's simply less distracting. Plain, bright colors are more stylish. So, a simple primary colored t-shirt with or

without a nice jacket or blazer is a safe option.
- **c)** Since the shots for a PTC are usually medium or close-up, you may not need to worry too much about your bottom half. But black pants or jeans are always a safe choice. Please avoid messy hair. Keep it tidy and avoid wearing anything on your hair like a face cap or a hoodie. A hoodie might be necessary though if you're reporting in the snow, otherwise keep your hair modest, you don't want anything to distract your audience from the story you're trying to tell.

EXERCISE

1) What's the significance of a PTC in a package?
A) To show off your beautiful face
B) To let your family know you're on TV
C) A PTC proves you were there, in the field, right where the story is going down.

MODULE 8: WRITING A SCRIPT

There are three basic aspects of a package that are equally important. The visuals, the sound – including your voice – and the story itself.

Learning how to write your story for broadcast is arguably the hardest part of the production process. It is a skill that takes a lot of practice and study to fully master. But learning is also a personal journey of trial and error which involves developing your own style with consideration of certain rules, including high standards of accurate, clear and concise writing.

Your facts must be facts, and you must write in a conversational tone, which is different from writing for print media. Broadcast TV writing style is direct, conversational, and easy to understand. It makes visual storytelling simple and relatable.

Take for example this first line from a New York Times article:
"A jury on Tuesday found Georgia men who murdered Ahmaud Arbery guilty of a federal hate crime, determining that they were motivated by racism when they chased the 25-year-old Black man through their neighborhood."

Brilliant first line for print. But it'll be a mouthful on TV. Here's one way you could rewrite that for a TV broadcast script, with corresponding visuals of course:

"Georgia jury declares convicted killers of Ahmaud Arbery guilty of a federal hate crime. The judge ruled Arbery was targeted because of the color of his skin."

Since starting out is usually the hardest part. I'll provide you with tips on how and where to start, a basic understanding of what makes a news script.

Here's a template for a script package. Nothing in here is cast in stone but is to give you a good idea of what your script should look like. A basic three-SOT news script structure looks like the following:

Intro/Pres

Take Pkg

Lede

Sot1

Nutgraph

Sot2

Sot3

Pay off

First Last Name, News Company, Location

Let's go over each section and talk a little about what goes where.

Intro/Pres
The first section is called the Intro or Pres—short for Presenter. It's meant to be read by the presenter and its purpose is to introduce your package before it airs. Think of it as a teaser for your story. When writing it, never give all the details away. It should be three to four sentences and between 20 and 30 seconds long. A good way to structure it is to establish the what, where and perhaps the who of your story. But leave the why out to be revealed in the package. The last line of the intro usually **creates a question** that can only be answered by watching the package itself.

Here's an example: *For decades, the world's (WHERE) glaciers (WHAT) have been melting at a rapid pace, driving a rise in global sea levels and weather disasters. Climate scientists (WHO) monitoring them warn that human activity is largely to blame. But as John Doe reports, glaciers are now melting so fast, it's getting harder and harder to study them.*

As the presenter reads this, the viewer is left asking: Why is it getting harder to study them? This example says a lot without mentioning that quick ice melt causes chunks to break off the glaciers, getting in the way of research boats.

After the Intro comes the first lines of the package, called the "lead-in" or the lede.

Lede

The lede in a broadcast is a bit like the lede in a print article. For breaking news, the first sentences of a package include the most important parts of the breaking or ongoing breaking story. The very first line can be a little expressive, but don't use adjectives. In fact, avoid all adjectives in your scripts until you're a pro and know what an editor will allow. And never describe what the viewer is seeing on the screen. They're already seeing it. Write to the picture.

Here's an example of a breaking news lede:

Video shows a burning garment factory with workers stuck inside.
"There's no escape from the flames for several workers at this clothing factory in Uganda."

The what, where, when, how, is quickly summarized in the next line, and then supported by the first SOT.

SOT1

The first SOT is very important, so choose it carefully. It should be short, dramatic, emotional and expressive. It should be a reaction of someone directly affected by the story, like a relative of someone stuck in the building. They can use adjectives too. They give credibility to your story and provide a human connection. Between each section, you should make sure you're using transitions from one to the next. Otherwise, they'll seem to float as separate entities. 'But' and 'and' are very simple examples of transitions. Instead of saying 'Molly has a bird. It is red. It needs food every day. It eats fruit.'... notice the transitions: "Molly has a bird. And it is red. It also needs food every day. And that food is usually fruit." This is essential in storytelling.

Nutgraph
The nutgraph is the paragraph with the heart of your story. It demonstrates why it deserves to be a story. It usually includes numbers with death tolls, famine, humanitarian need, and stories with a wide impact on humans. International news stories almost always do.

An example: *Remember the factory fire LEDE? Imagine it was followed by a SOT from a survivor, shot at a safe distance from the building still on fire, or the smoldering ruins. She describes what she saw, how she escaped, if she saw anyone hurt or injured or even killed.*

If the story were about frequent fires in factories, you might find data from an NGO or an aid organization on how often it happens. If it were a story about unsafe conditions in a sweatshop setting, the nutgraph might report statements directly from survivor interviews, combined with images/video they took as proof.

If three major fashion brands were found to be working with this factory, it might be data on what percentage of fast fashion is estimated to be made in dangerous factories/sweatshops. It's the strongest evidence that what you're reporting is relevant, and for international news, it's also the strongest evidence that it has a wide impact. It's concrete numbers, or facts, backed by experts.

SOT2

The second SOT after the nutgraph, has one job and only one job to do – verify the information you provided in the nutgraph. It could be a survivor talking about dangerous conditions. It could be an NGO spokesperson talking about how vulnerable factories in Uganda are to fires. Or about how often big brands hire sweatshops to produce their clothes. You could also switch it up and use a SOT from a representative of one of the brands accused of hiring the factory. This person is likely to defend and or say something about what the company is doing or preparing to do to avoid such a disaster in the future. Sometimes, they might even deny culpability. Either way, you must give the accused the opportunity to respond for fairness and balance.

Between SOT2 and SOT3 is where you can add extra evidence to support your nutgraph. Or you can add interest to the story. It can be an extra angle. You could talk about the working conditions in the factory and wages. Or about a faulty inspection process or lack of inspections. If you do that, then…

SOT3

The third SOT backs up what you said in the previous section. If you've already used an official, and it's a feature story, I like to use another survivor. Some stories use survivors for all three SOTS. Some use officials for all three SOTS. It's flexible, but the way you choose to tell it has to make sense with the story.

SOT3 is also a great place for a PTC. Your PTC can also come at the end of your package. And it can serve the same function, backing up or adding interest by expanding on a story with something extra. Don't try to shove three SOTS and a PTC into your early scripts. It's a lot, and requires experience to pull it off successfully. Remember, most scripts are a minute and a half to two minutes long.

The Payoff

And the last section is the payoff. They are tricky for many producers. Some quickly become payoff masters, others leave it to the very last thing they write. There's no real guidance on where you have to start your script. Some start with the intro, some leave it for the last. It's about your own comfort level as a writer.

The point of a payoff is to leave the viewers feeling like the time they passed watching your package was worth it. A good payoff keeps the viewers engaged with the story long after they have stopped seeing it. It wraps up the story but with a hint about the future.

Here are some tips for writing a good payoff. You can use some or all of these tips to start writing good payoffs.

a) You may choose to close the story the way you started, by returning to the impact of the conflict on your characters
b) Keep it human
c) Suggest possibilities

Let's use the factory fire as an example. A good payoff for the story could be: *"These survivors escaped once, but without worker's rights they could find themselves in mortal danger, again."*

Sign Off

Once you're done with your script, don't forget to add your sign-off. It's how you finish. Say your first and last names, followed by the company name and the location you're reporting. If you're not in the field, that is if you're filing a package in the newsroom, usually without a PTC, then your location is not required.

For example, I would say: *"Adesewa Josh, CNN, or Adesewa Josh, CNN, Lagos, Nigeria."*

EXERCISE

Identify the intro, lede, nutgraph, PTC, and pay-off in this sample script:

Tennis ace Novak Djokovic has hit the court in Australia, but not the type of court he's used to. The Serbian star has launched a legal challenge to the cancellation of his Australian visa. Djokovic has refused to say whether or not he's fully vaccinated against COVID 19. He was granted a medical exemption to play at the Australian Open, but was then denied entry when he landed in Melbourne. John Doe has the latest.

[Van driving into a hotel]

Smuggled into a quarantined hotel in a blacked-out van, and flanked by staff in PPEs...
This isn't the Australian welcome the world's number one tennis star was expecting.

SOT - Scott Morrison - Australian Prime Minister
"Rules are rules. And there are no special cases. Rules are rules."

(Novak file Photos)
Novak Djokovic proudly boasted on social media that he'd been granted a medical exemption to enter the country to defend his Australian Open title.

[Police cars on tarmac]

But when his plane touched down, the police were waiting for him.

SOT - Greg Hunt - Australian Health Minister
"Mr Djokovic failed to provide appropriate evidence to meet

the entry requirements to Australia, and his visa has been subsequently canceled."

[Novak at the airport]
It is believed he spent eight hours at the airport challenging the decision, before launching a Federal Court appeal.

Since not everyone is the world's top tennis player, Novak Djokovic's visa cancellation has been attracting huge international attention. Earlier this week, news of his medical exemption sparked an outcry in Australia.

[Novak supporters]

But now it' s revocation has caused considerable anger.

VOX POP
"It's not fair. It's discriminating against him, just because he chooses not to state his vax status. I mean, it's a personal choice."

On the other hand, Serbia's President Aleksandar Vucic has described Djokovic's treatment as harassment. But the Australian Government says, everyone has to play by the same rules.

John Doe, ABC News, XYZ

MODULE 9: VOICING

So, you've written a script and it's been approved by editors and an executive producer. The next step is voicing.

It's a very important part of your package. Voicing can get your audience to tune in, or turn off their screens. Your tone of voice must be as interesting as your story. Avoid animating your voice too much when reading your script. It's distracting. Narrate your story like you're speaking to a friend, but here's the twist…use a tone of voice that mirrors the emotions of your story without being melodramatic.

Voicing is an art that requires smooth delivery and emphasis on the key points in your story. While it can be taught, it takes practice to really get good at it and to find your own unique voice and rhythm. Please do not try to sound like someone else. It's the worst thing you can do to yourself.

Here are some tips:

Practice your script.
Read your script out loud several times to get familiar with it and get over any bumps in your delivery during practice – not while you're recording. Keep an eye out for words that are going to be hard to pronounce, or ones that you might stumble over. Repeat those words out loud until you feel comfortable with their pronunciation. Do deep breathing exercises by breathing in quickly and deeply several times, and being sure to force out all the air.

Identify the operative words
These are the most important words in a phrase or sentence. These are words which, all by themselves, would still give the

listener the gist of the story. They're the words the listener needs to hear to stay with the story. Read through your script and underline or highlight them. They're usually the classic who-what-where-when-why-how words – nouns, adjectives, adverbs, titles, names. e.g: *He was a painter – "was" being the operative word.*

Emphasize the operative words
Once you've identified the keywords that tell your story, you need to slightly emphasize those words when reading your script.

You do that in these four ways:

a) **Volume** – Modulate your voice by raising or lowering the volume of your voice, depending on the word and context. Emphasizing a word by making your voice louder is also called "punching" it. For example: *"Carrie took refuge under her bed when she heard a LOUD bang on her balcony at midnight on Sunday"*... you should give a slight punch to the word 'loud'. Not in a melodramatic way, but for emphasis.

b) **Pitch** – Change the pitch of your voice when you say an operative word. I must warn you that this is a very tricky part, as most people sound like phonies when pitch is misplaced or misused, or even overused. You want to sound as natural and authentic as possible. My personal rule is to just practice, practice, practice. After a while, you'll find your rhythm.

c) **Rhythm** – Is how you space your words when saying an operative word. Pause before the word, or after the word, or both, to emphasize it. A pause is especially effective before a word that's complex or highly technical in nature. A pause is also effective when you're introducing a new idea in a script.

d) **Tempo** – Don't rush your script, but at the same time please don't put us to bed. Find a way to pace yourself through the script. This is an art, you'll develop your unique tempo through practice.

e) **Delivery** – This is about breath work. Besides marking the operative words for emphasis, you also need to mark your breaths on your script, this helps you know where you're going to pause to take a breath. Longer sentences are going to need a breath, usually taken where a comma appears in the script or where new information is introduced. The trick is to sound like you're having a conversation with someone, not like you're reading from a script or lecturing. *Tell* the story, don't read it.

Think about how you would tell it to a group of friends, then adopt that tone when reading your script. Stay in the story while you're reading it. Think about what you're saying.

In the sound booth, keep your mouth parallel to the mic – avoid looking down as that affects the sound of your voice. Let your voice mildly mirror the emotions of your scripted story, and that's all the animation required for voicing a news story.

Finally, take a pause after your pay-off … before you sign off … or when you say your name in your package. Pronounce your name clearly. Give the listener an opportunity to remember it. This is quite important since your story's likely going to be broadcast to an international audience.

MODULE 10: EDITING

A 21st-century reporter must be able to edit at least the rough-cut of their package. This is a great skill to have, not just because it's a requirement of most international newsrooms, but also because it puts less pressure on the remote craft/video editor who's most likely an employee of the international newsroom you're working with.

Being able to edit your rough-cut from the field gives the craft editor a better understanding of the visual direction of your story. If they edit from scratch, it's cumbersome. They may not have the patience to select the best shots, or choose the shots you like, since they weren't in the field with you.

There are two widely used video editing applications in the industry: Edius and Premiere Pro. This module isn't about how to use these softwares (I recommend you take a separate editing class for this) but what to look out for when editing your package. The trick to editing is to follow the script you've written and only change it when you absolutely must. Here is a guideline on how to layer your package.

     i. You must begin and end every story with natural sound. Start editing by putting your voiced script on the audio channel of the timeline. Edit the voice to take out any repeats, spaces, and breaths, and put them in sequence.

     ii. Then start laying the visuals as described in your script. Give at least three seconds of up-sound/natural sound at the beginning of your first shot; it should be your best picture, just before we hear your narration.

iii. Allow appropriate pauses to follow your sentences. And use natural sound. Include a natural sound break before and after sound bites. Of course, the natural sound has to be relevant to what the interview is discussing.
iv. Following the sequence in your script, insert your sots in the appropriate places. Finally allow a brief second of natural sound after your signoff to end the package. Also, do not forget to end the package with your second-best picture.

Now, it's time to publish your amazing story with the world. But please wait till its first broadcast by the news organization. Don't get so excited to share that you break the network's broadcast guidelines. The broadcast process differs from one news organization to another, so it's always good to know the network you're working with.

Ask the planning producer you're corresponding with on your story for the deadline. If you're working remotely or as a freelancer, you'll be required to transfer your package to the network's media pool. Two good applications for that is WeTransfer and SendGB. They're the simplest way to send your files around the world, and you can transfer up to 2GB and 5GB respectively, free at a go. There's also Dropbox, which is a cloud storage service. It also has a free version, but most people prefer WeTransfer or SendGB because they don't require you to register for an account.

Lastly, make yourself visible. Know when the organization will air your story. Tell everyone you know to watch it, and talk about it on your social media platforms. Check if the organization will post your story online. This is a great opportunity for visibility, as it makes other potential clients easily find your work online.

Good luck!

Made in the USA
Coppell, TX
08 January 2024